Y0-DOK-326

My Heart, Christ's Home

100 Days of Joy and Strength in Jesus

Patricia Adderley

Copyright © 2022 by Patricia Adderley

ISBN: 9798363761416

Imprint: Independently published. All Rights Reserved.

No portion of this book may be reproduced in any form without written permission from the publisher or author, except as permitted by U.S. copyright law.

All scriptures are taken from THE HOLY BIBLE, NEW INTERNATIONAL VERSION ®, NIV ® Copyright ©1973, 1978, 1984, 2011 by Biblica, Inc. TM Used by permission. All rights reserved worldwide.

For a Limited Time, Get a Free Copy of My Book

Finding Peace in Jesus: An Encouraging 30 Day Devotional

https://dl.bookfunnel.com/nl4rxrd4oh

Also By Patricia Adderley

https://patriciaadderley.com/my-writing/

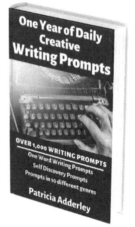

Contents

To My Wonderful Husband, John, who loves me unconditionally and supports me in all that I do.

Introduction

My Heart, Christ's Home is a collection of 100 poems and the scriptures they were based on. God lives inside each one of us, if we've accepted Him as our Savior. However, Salvation is only the beginning of a lifelong journey. Throughout our lives, we will face trials of many kinds. We have to deal with loss and grief, fear, faith, or questions of identity just to name a few.

We ask ourselves things like *"Does God really know me?"*, *"Who did God create me to be?"* or *"Is there more to life than this job?"*.

We hide things about ourselves from other people and, especially, from God. We are afraid that if they found out who we really are we might be rejected. Whether warranted or not, we feel shame for our past actions, feelings, and thoughts.

I don't know about you, but it' a constant process to turn over those hidden parts of my heart and mind to God. This life is only the beginning of all that God has for us. He has a purpose for each one of us. Additionally, He wants access to every part of our lives- where we work, where we live and eat, the bedroom and the closets where we hide things. Everything.

How many of us accept His gift of salvation and then never really take time to pursue a deeper relationship with Him? We can trust Him with every part of our lives- good or bad. That's part of what the Psalms are about. These are moments where David cried out to God. He confessed his sins, expressed his doubs and fears, and his faith in God. He worshipped God and praised Him

That's what this collection of 100 poems are about also. They are moments in time where I asked God many of the questions I listed here and more. As I take time to be with Him and listen to Him, He fills me with His peace. I find rest from my anxious thoughts. He shows me who He created me to be and He gives me strength. No matter what the circumstances, He fills me with unspeakable joy.

He can do the same for you as well. As you read this, I encourage you to take time to listen to God. My hope is that this book will be a resources that can help you draw closer to God. He has great plans for your live, even if at moments it doesn't seem like it. He just wants to be with you. He wants you to turn to Him with all of your prayers, thoughts, hopes and dreams. He's waiting.

Patricia Adderley

ONE

Accepted

"As Scripture says, 'Anyone who believes in him will never be put to shame.' for there is no difference between Jews and Gentiles- the same Lord is Lord of all and richly blesses all who call on him, for, 'Everyone who calls on the name of the Lord will be saved.'" **Romans 10:11**

Rejected by man

But saved from above.

Accepted by God and

Secure in His love.

No matter my sins,

I am safe in His arms.

His mercy is enough.

He protects me from harm.

He raises me up

Higher than an eagle's wings.

As my spirit soars,

I sing praises to my King.

I lay down my life.

Serving Him each day

Created on purpose

To follow His way.

Two

All Creation Sings

"The heavens declare the glory of God; the skies proclaim the work of his hands. Day after day they pour forth speech; night after night they reveal knowledge." **Psalms 19: 1-2**

So much creativity

In the world I see.

The brilliant blue skies

And the deep blue seas.

Huge Rocky Mountains

And green rolling hills.

The hot desert sands

And sunsets that thrill.

The warm summer nights

And the cool ocean breeze

The stars in the skies

And the leaves on the trees.

The birds in the air

And the fish in the sea.

Elephants and lions

And whales of the deep.

Everywhere I look

There's beauty to be found.

There's surely a God

With all that's around.

All creation sings of His glory.

All creation tells His story.

Surely, He is good

And His mercy everlasting.

Love never-ending

And glory forever shining.

THREE

All Things Are Possible

"I can do all things through him who gives me strength." **Philippians 4:13**

In You, Lord

All things are possible.

There is nothing

That cannot be accomplished

When we trust in you.

You give us strength

When we are weak.

When we don't know who we are,

You remind us that we are yours.

When we step off the cliff in faith,

Your hand is there to catch us

And to help us fly.

In you, we can rise on wings like eagles.

We can keep on running

To finish the race.

We can face all obstacles.

We can face all trials

Knowing that you are

Right there with us

Holding us and strengthening us,

Showing us how to draw on

The power of your Holy Spirit.

Never will you leave us.

Never will you forsake us.

Forever we are yours

Through the wonderful,

Cleansing blood of Jesus.

The Word become Flesh, Savior,

Comforter and Coming King.

Four

As the Birds Chirp and Fly

"So do not worry, saying, 'What shall we eat?' or 'What shall we drink?' or 'What shall we wear?' For the pagans run after all these things, and your heavenly Father knows that you need them." **Matthew 6:31**

As the birds chirp and fly

From tree to tree,

They don't worry

About tomorrow.

As the lilies grow

In the fields with

All their brilliant colors,

They don't worry about

God's provision.

As the dolphins

Dance in the sea,

Their hearts are free

To be who God

Created them to be-

Without worry,

Without care.

Lay your burdens down.

Don't worry about tomorrow.

God has things in control.

Let your heart find rest

Under the shadow of His arms.

FIVE

At The End

"Never will I leave you; never will I forsake you." **Hebrews 13:5b**

When I'm at the end

Of all I know to do,

I lean into the Lord

And listen, for I know

He sees me through.

As I try to quiet my heart

And silence my racing thoughts,

I tune my heart to His voice.

For He always has the answers.

And always fills me with peace.

"I've got your back",

He says,

"I'll never let you down".

One step at a time,

I'll lead you through.

Six

Be The Light

"Do not gloat over me, my enemy! Though I have fallen, I will rise. Though I sit in darkness, the LORD will be my light." **Micah 7:8**

Created by God.

Filled with His love.

Filled with His light.

Hidden by shadows, thorns & trials.

Weighed down by darkness

It seeks to smother the light.

Not possible!

Just remember your creator.

Just remember your Savior.

Be the light as He is the light.

Surrender to His voice.

Surrender to His love.

True unconditional love

Is the light.

Don't fight the darkness.

Shine a light and dispel the darkness.

Be Jesus to a lost and dying world.

SEVEN

Beware

"Finally, be strong in the Lord and in his mighty power. Put on the full armor of God, so that you can take your stand against the devil's schemes. For our struggle is not against flesh and blood, but against the rulers, against the authorities, against the powers of this dark world and against the spiritual forces of evil in the heavenly realms." **Ephesians 6:10-12**

Beware the enemy!

He comes with cunning and power.

He'll deceive you and lie to you

And seek whom He can devour.

Beware the enemy!

Make sure to keep up your guard.

Stand firm in God's strength

For you, He'll fight hard.

He'll never let you go

And He'll help you win the fight.

Just keep your eyes on Him

Let Him be your light.

He's given you all the weapons

That you'll ever need.

The belt of truth,

The breastplate of righteousness

And the Gospel of Peace.

The Helmut of Salvation

And the Shield of Faith.

The Sword of the Spirit

Which is the Word of God.

The prayer offered in faith

Will help you stand,

Trusting the battle

To God's mighty hands.

EIGHT

The Body of Christ

"Remain in me, as I also remain in you. No branch can bear fruit by itself; it must remain in the vine. Neither can you bear fruit unless you remain in me. I am the vine; you are the branches. If you remain in me and I in you, you will bear much fruit; apart from me you can do nothing. If you do not remain in me, you are like a branch that is thrown away and withers; such branches are picked up, thrown into the fire and burned. If you remain in me and my words remain in you, ask whatever you wish, and it will be done for you." **John 15: 4-7**

We are the body of Christ.

No two exactly the same.

I am unique and so are you.

Made on purpose to glorify His name.

We are the branches

And He is the Vine,

The source of all life.

Without Him, we can do nothing.

One is a teacher

And another is a prophet.

All equally needed and called

To share His great light

To neighbors and strangers,

Family and friends.

Wherever you are

Share the love that never ends.

Step out in faith.

He'll be with you

Each step of the way.

Let him lead you.

He'll teach you what to say.

Be confident, be bold.

There's power in Jesus' name.

The lives that you touch

Will never be the same.

NINE

Christmas Joy

"'Sovereign Lord, as you have promised, you may now dismiss your servant in peace. For my eyes have seen your salvation, which you have prepared in the sight of all nations: a light for revelation to the Gentiles, and the glory of your people Israel.'" **Luke 2:29-32**

Christmas trees

Pointing to heaven,

Sparkling with lights

That glimmer

Like the stars.

Mary and Joseph

And baby Jesus

In the manger.

Presents under the trees,

Hot chocolate

And sugar cookies

In the kitchen.

Family and friends

Under the mistletoe.

Thankfulness and giving

Because of the One

Who gave it all-

That first Christmas day.

TEN

Come Dine with Me

"Here I am! I stand at the door and knock. If anyone hears my voice and opens the door, I will come in and eat with that person, and they with me." **Revelation 3:20**

Come dine with me.

Let's have a great meal

Of bread and wine

And forgiveness for sin.

Come walk with me

In the garden and by the sea.

We'll have a great talk,

Just you and me.

Come work with me side by side.

Let's see what we can do.

With a heart fully surrendered,

There's nothing we can't do.

Come join me in heaven.

We'll laugh and rejoice.

No more pain, death, or disease

With me forevermore.

Come to the table

That I've prepared for you.

The bread of forgiveness,

The wine of release.

ELEVEN

Created on Purpose

"Your eyes saw my unformed body; all the days ordained for me were written in your book before one of them came to be." **Psalm 139: 16**

I'm significant, secure

And safe in His love.

He created me on purpose

And He has a plan.

Before I was born,

He knew my name.

Created my soul and spirit

Deep within me.

He ordained all my days

Before one of them

Came to be.

Molds me on His potter's wheel

Into who He wants me to be.

He created me for a relationship

To eternally be with Him.

To share His love

Which shines from within.

He created me to be unique

There's no one else like me.

I am not a copy

Nor should I be.

I am not a mistake

But was planned before time began

To good works together

With my best friend.

TWELVE

Do You Hear It?

"Then a great and powerful wind tore the mountains apart and shattered the rocks before the Lord, but the Lord was not in the wind. After the wind there was an earthquake, but the Lord was not in the earthquake. After the earthquake came a fire, but the Lord was not in the fire. And after the fire came a gentle whisper." **1 Kings 19:11b-12**

Shhh. Be quiet.

Do you hear it?

A still small voice

But a whisper it is.

You must be quiet

Or you will miss it.

Full of love and truth,

Wisdom and strength

As gentle as the breeze

And as strong as the wind.

Never forced.

Waiting for you.

Waiting for me.

Patiently.

Lovingly.

Ready to tell me

Great and unsearchable

Things that I do not know.

THIRTEEN

Don't Give Up

"And my God will meet all your needs according to the riches of his glory in Christ Jesus." **Philippians 4:19**

Don't give up.

Don't give in.

The Holy Spirit

Will help you win.

"The fight is mine."

Says the Lord.

"Just trust in me,

Forevermore."

"I'll walk with you

And talk with you

And provide for

All your needs.

I'll teach you

And guide you

As you draw close

And let me lead."

Fourteen

Driving Along

"However, I consider my life worth nothing to me; my only aim is to finish the race and complete the task the Lord Jesus has given me- the task of testifying to the good news of God's grace." **Acts 20:24**

Driving along

Without a care in the world

Watching the clouds drift by.

Wondering at the grace

That so captured my heart,

Giving thanks and praise

To the One and Only God.

My heart sings

Sweet melodies of peace and joy.

Thankful for forgiveness

And of all that held me bound.

Now I am free

To serve and to praise.

Free like the wind

As I drive along

This road of life.

Wondering what He

May have next for me.

One adventure after another.

Driving along

With the wind in my face

Until that wondrous day

When he calls me

To my eternal home.

Fifteen

Enlarge The Place of Your Tent

"Enlarge the place of your tent, stretch your tent curtains wide, do not hold back; lengthen your cords, strengthen your stakes." **Isaiah 54:2**

"Enlarge the place of your tent."

Open wide the gates.

Stretch, challenge, listen.

Holy Spirit come in.

Let's do this together.

One step toward you

And one step toward me.

Hand in hand we walk

Doing life together.

Steps of faith.

Outside my comfort zone.

Flying on Eagle's wings

As you lead me,

Stretch me,

Help me to grow,

Becoming all that you

Created me to be.

With you, not for you.

Loving and praising you

With all my heart and all my mind.

May my life be a symphony

Of your glory

Working through me.

Sixteen

Fear Has Been Defeated

"Have I not commanded you? Be strong and courageous. Do not be afraid; do not be discouraged for the Lord your God will be with you wherever you go." **Joshua 1:9**

Fear has been defeated.

It no longer has a hold.

It was defeated on the cross

And was buried in the grave.

Fear no longer controls me.

Freedom in Christ reigns.

No need to fear tomorrow.

God sees all and knows all.

Nothing is a surprise.

Walk confidently in Him

Trusting Him to lead the way.

He knows the pitfalls

And will make the way clear.

He'll walk with you

Through the valleys,

Up the mountainside,

And through every river.

He'll carry you

And walk with you

Side by side.

No fear can control you.

No fear can hold you

With Jesus at your side.

SEVENTEEN

Fill Your Heart

"For God, who said, 'Let light shine out of darkness,' made his light shine in our hearts to give us the light of the knowledge of God's glory displayed in the face of Christ." **2 Corinthians 4:6**

Anger, cruelty, jealousy

Invades our towns and

Takes over our communities.

But it doesn't have to be.

Let Him fill your heart

With His peace.

Let your spirit soar.

Let your heart sing.

Share His love

With people far and wide.

Kindness, gentleness

Let Him speak from inside.

It doesn't take much

To turn things around.

A softly spoken word

Or a selfless gesture.

Put others first.

What you give you shall receive.

Let His light shine

And the darkness can't stay.

His joy and peace will come

And darkness will go away.

Eighteen

Finish the Race

"Enter through the narrow gate. For wide is the gate and broad is the road that leads to destruction, and many enter through it. But small is the gate and narrow the road that leads to life, and only a few find it." **Matthew 7:13-14**

Run, walk, fall,

Pick yourself back up again

To run again.

Finish the race

With the wind of the Holy Spirit

Leading you,

Guiding you

Showing you the way.

The narrow way,

Just one path.

Reaching higher, deeper.

Listen to the still small voice within

Words of hope, love,

Guidance, peace.

Nineteen

For Where Your Treasure Is

"Do not store up for yourselves treasures on earth, where moths and vermin destroy, and where thieves break in and steal. But store up for yourselves treasures in heaven, where moths and vermin do not destroy, and where thieves do not break in and steal. For where your treasure is, there your heart will be also." **Matthew 6:19-21**

Where is my heart?

On what does it cling?

Treasures on earth

Or, on those from above?

Money, power, fame?

Or love, heart, and grace?

Looks and status?

Or Justice and truth?

Search your heart.

What's on the inside?

Let God show you,

Cleanse you,

Purify you.

In your heart

Let Him abide.

TWENTY

Forever Thankful

"I will give thanks to you, Lord, with all my heart; I will tell of all your wonderful deeds. I will be glad and rejoice in you; I will sing the praises of your name, O Most High." **Psalms 9:1-2**

Lord, I am forever thankful

For the sun and the moon

And the stars in the skies.

The planets in the heavens

And the beauty of the night.

Lord, I am forever thankful

For the bird's beautiful songs

And kittens at play.

The loving devotion of dogs

And the dawn of a new day.

Lord, I am forever thankful

For hugs and kisses from my love

And the light in His eyes.

The laughter from within

As it spontaneously arises.

Lord, I am forever thankful

For clouds in the skies

And mountains and streams.

Rivers and lush green valleys

And all created things.

Lord, I am forever thankful

For chocolate and ice cream,

Delicious meals of pizza or pasta

And other wonderful delicacies.

Lord, I am forever thankful,

Most importantly of all,

For mercy, salvation, and grace,

Forgiveness of sins

And filling me with faith.

TWENTY-ONE

Gifts

"Every good and perfect gift is from above, coming down from the Father of the heavenly lights, who does not change like shifting shadows." **James 1: 17**

So many gifts

Are sent from above.

His mercy and grace

And Sacrificial love.

Forgiveness and

Healing,

Joy and laughter,

And purpose in living.

The sound of singing birds

And the laughter of a child.

Hugs and kisses

From special people

And a smile from a stranger.

Puppies and kittens at play

And Squirrels scurrying up trees.

The soft gentle breeze

On a hot summer day,

Or a roaring fire

In the middle of winter.

So many gifts

Sent from Father God

Above.

Endless blessings

And His Never-ending Love.

TWENTY-TWO

God Almighty

"For in him all things were created: things in heaven and on earth, visible and invisible, whether thrones or power or rulers or authorities; all things have been created through him and for him. He is before all things, and in him all things hold together." **Colossians 1:16-17**

He's Almighty God

Creator of the universe,

Word become Flesh.

Everything began with Him-

The stars in the heavens

And the oceans so vast.

He separated day and night,

Raised the mountains,

And painted the sky.

Beautiful, ever-changing colors

Each day and night.

Created the wind-

Strong and yet gentle.

The lion with its mighty roar

And the tiny meow of my kitty.

The laughing hyena

And the bark of the dog.

The fish that swims in the sea

And the leaping frog.

The beautiful fragrance of a rose

And the fruit on the tree.

Everything in all creation,

Including you and me.

Twenty-Three

God's Faithfulness

"He will cover you with his feathers, and under his wings you will find refuge; his faithfulness will be your shield and rampart." **Psalms 91:4**

God's faithfulness

Is my shield.

I am protected

On every side.

His Word is my sword

With which I protect

My heart and mind.

His Spirit lives within me,

Guiding me each day.

His truth is in me.

His righteousness shields me.

As I abide in Him,

He protects me on every side

From all known calamities.

I am secure and safe

In His arms.

I am surrounded

By His love.

TWENTY-FOUR

Hallelujah! He is Risen!

"he will swallow up death forever. The Sovereign Lord will wipe away the tears from all faces; he will remove his people's disgrace from all the earth. The Lord has spoken. In that day they will say, 'Surely this is our God; we trusted in him, and he saved us. This is the Lord, we trusted in him; let us rejoice and be glad in his salvation.'" **Isaiah 25:8-9**

Hallelujah! He has Risen!

Hallelujah for the Son!

Hallelujah, He died and rose again.

Praise God new life's begun.

Hallelujah for the father!

Hallelujah for the son!

Hallelujah our home's in heaven!

Praise Him three in one.

He's the One and Only Father

Of the One and Only Son.

He's the Spirit deep within me

And I'm singing a new song.

Hallelujah, He conquered death!!

Hallelujah, He conquered hell!

Hallelujah, I am born again!

Praise the Father of us all.

TWENTY-FIVE

He Is the Light

"This is the message we have heard from Him and declare to you: God is Light; in Him there is no darkness at all." **1 John 1:5**

He's the light in the darkness,

The savior of all mankind.

My friend and my redeemer,

My Lord and my king.

I'll serve Him forever

No matter how hard.

For, He's always there when I need Him

And He knows what is best.

He called me to serve him

Before I even knew Him.

And, I can never say no to my God

For He love me so much.

He suffered and died for me and rose again.

Conquering death and sin

And washing me clean.

TWENTY-SIX

Heart Songs

"Shout for joy to the Lord, all the earth. Worship the Lord with gladness; come before him with joyful songs." **Psalms 100: 1-2**

My heart leaps for joy

In praise to my King.

Inexpressible heart songs

Of thankfulness and peace.

His love overwhelms me

Like a cup that overflows.

I laugh for joy.

Circumstances don't matter.

He's totally faithful.

Totally trustworthy.

No more worries-

Just peace, hope, and joy.

He's worthy of all praise.

Worthy of my trust.

He lifts me up

And hides me

Under the shelter

Of His wings.

In Him I fly

Under the power of His love.

Joy unspeakable.

Joy unimaginable.

Overflowing.

Spilling over

To Jesus, loving Savior

Do I forever sing His praise.

TWENTY-SEVEN

Hearts of Glass

"The Lord is close to the brokenhearted and saves those who are crushed in spirit. The righteous person may have many troubles, but the Lord delivers him from them all." **Psalms 34:18-19**

Hearts of glass.

Fragile.

Easily broken.

Got to protect it,

Keep it from shattering.

Lies.

Let God break through.

Open your heart.

Let His Love heal.

Let his forgiveness in.

Don't keep the pain inside.

Release it all

Into His strong, safe hands.

He is trustworthy.

He will keep you safe.

Let His light fill

The dark recesses of your heart.

Let His love overflow.

TWENTY-EIGHT

Heaven

"The twelve gates were twelve pearls, each gate made of a single pearl.
The great street of the city was of gold, as pure as transparent glass."
Revelation 21:21

Heaven,

Our eternal home.

Gates of solid pearls,

Walls garnished

With precious jewels,

And streets of pure gold.

No sun or moon

For the glory of God

Is its light.

No sin or evil

No pain, disease, or death

Exists here.

It's gone-

Forever.

Only heavenly perfection.

Love, joy, and peace.

His everlasting forgiveness,

His mercy and grace.

Forever with Him

In heavenly paradise.

TWENTY-NINE

Heavenly Father

"God said to Moses, 'I AM WHO I AM.' This is what you are to say to the Israelites: 'I AM has sent me to you.'" **Exodus 3:14**

He's the Word become Flesh

It all started with Him.

Almighty God,

El Shaddai,

Creator of the Universe.

He's my Heavenly Father,

Daddy God,

My best friend.

Holy Spirit.

Strong as the ocean

Gentle as the breeze.

Deep within.

He's inside me

All around me

Lifting me up

And leading the way

He's Jesus Christ,

Loving Savior,

Returning King.

He sits on the throne

Preparing a home,

Coming soon for you and me.

THIRTY

His Love is Sufficient

"But he said to me, 'My grace is sufficient for you, for my power is made perfect in weakness.' Therefore, I will boast all the more gladly of my weaknesses, so that the power of Christ may rest upon me." **2 Corinthians 12:9**

When you have no more strength

And it's more than you can bear,

Turn to the Lord

And He'll hear your prayer.

He'll give you the strength you need

And will truly carry you through.

For, His love is sufficient

And will see you through.

You may not see the difference

Between His will and your own.

But, if you seek him out first,

He'll make the answer known.

It's sometimes difficult

To respond to His call.

But when you place your faith in Him,

He will never let you fall.

When you're lost and confused

About which way is right,

Just keep your eyes on Him

And He'll be your light.

THIRTY-ONE

Hope Arises

"Here is a trustworthy saying that deserves full acceptance: Christ Jesus came into the world to save sinners- of whom I am the worst." **1 Timothy 1:15**

Hope arises

As I ponder

Your great love.

You conquered

Death and sin

After descending

From above.

Born of a virgin

An innocent babe,

Dependent on man

For all your needs.

You spoke words

Of love and truth

To all who would listen,

Were betrayed

And were crucified,

And then rose again.

You conquered death and sin

To save my soul,

To bring me home

So that I can forever

Be with you.

THIRTY-TWO

How Do I Thank You?

"Then Jesus came to them and said, 'All authority in heaven and on earth has been given to me. Therefore go and make disciples of all nations, baptizing them in the name of the Father and of the Son and of the Holy Spirit, and teaching them to obey everything I have commanded you. And surely I am with you always, to the very end of the age.'" **Matthew 28:18-20**

Lord, how do I thank you

For your love and sacrifice for us?

It's impossible.

You send us prophets and teachers

But we don't listen.

You create a beautiful world for us

In which to live

And we destroy it.

You call us by our name

And we take yours in vain.

You feed us and clothe us

And we give in to gluttony and greed.

You send us your son Jesus

And we kill him.

You raise him from the dead

And we find excuses not to believe.

You do miracles in your name

And we give Satan credit.

You give us your Word

And we ignore it.

Lord, we are so sinful

Yet you loved us so much

That you sacrificed your son.

Lord give us willing

And obedient hearts.

Strengthen us and equip us

To carry out your Holy commission,

To spread the gospel message

Through all the nations.

THIRTY-THREE

I AM

"I am the Living One; I was dead, and now look, I am alive for ever and ever! And I hold the keys of death and Hades." **Revelation 1: 18**

I'm Your Savior and Redeemer.

I'm your coming King.

I'll love you

And protect you

And show you the way.

You're my child.

I want to bless you.

I want to work with you

Side by side.

Sharing my love

As in me you abide.

I'm your father

And provider.

I am your best friend.

No matter what you do

My love will never end.

I'm the burning bush

And that still small voice

The Holy Spirit deep within

I'll continue to guide you

As you lean in and listen

I am your El Shaddai

I'm your daddy God

And will be with you

Till the end.

THIRTY-FOUR

I Wonder

"Who has measured the waters in the hollow of his hand or with the breadth of his hand marked off the heavens? Who has held the dust of the earth in a basket, or weighed the mountains on the scales and the hills in a balance?" **Isaiah 40:12**

I wonder that there are

So many stars in the heavens.

Or, why the earth is

The perfect distance from the sun,

Supporting a vast variety of life.

I wonder that no two sunsets

Are exactly alike.

I wonder that birds can fly

And Parrots can mimic speech.

I wonder that the grass is green

And the sky is blue.

The mountains so high and majestic

And the ocean so vast.

I wonder why each of us is so unique

Or that Zebras have stripes

And Leopards have spots.

I wonder that fire is hot

And ice is cold.

Surely, God has a great sense of humor

And unending imagination-

Just look at His creation.

THIRTY-FIVE

I'm a Child of God

"For you created my inmost being; you knit me together in my mother's womb. I praise you because I am fearfully and wonderfully made; your works are wonderful, I know that full well. My frame was not hidden from you when I was made in the secret place, when I was woven together in the depths of the earth." **Psalms 139: 13-15**

I'm a child of God

Daughter of the Most High,

A Princess in His Kingdom.

Created to fly.

Adopted by faith.

Received by grace.

Created for His purpose,

Unique in every way.

Loved, forgiven,

Chosen to share His light.

Called by the Father

Who gives me strength to fight.

I have a heavenly home.

I am beloved by my Groom.

I'm the bride of Christ

And I'm going home soon.

Purified through His blood,

Redeemed through His sacrifice,

Made holy for an eternity,

Reigning with my King.

THIRTY-SIX

I'm Singing a Silent Melody

"Because your love is better than life, my lips will glorify you. I will praise you as long as I live, and in your name I will lift up my hands." **Psalms 63: 3-4**

I'm singing a silent melody of praises to my king

Of love and joy and peace and praise

To Jesus Christ, Almighty God,

My Savior do I sing.

I'm singing a silent melody of praises to my Lord-

Thankfulness for forgiveness, healing and peace

To my loving Savior, the great I Am

Does my heart forever sing.

I'll sing in the morning and I'll sing when the day is done.

I'll worship and sing praises to Him

Today and every day, forever throughout eternity

To my Redeemer and my King.

Thirty-Seven

In the Stillness of the Night

"This is what the Lord says- your Redeemer, who formed you in the womb: 'I am the Lord, the Maker of all things, who stretches out the heavens, who spreads out the earth by myself," **Isaiah 44:24**

In the Stillness of the Night,

A voice whispers my name.

The same voice that called

The heavens into being,

The same voice that commanded

"Let there be light",

Spoke MY name.

He knows me.

He knows my innermost being.

Words of love,

Encouragement and strength.

The same God that created the stars,

The same God that raised the mountains,

Created ME.

Gave me purpose.

Talks to me.

So much love-

Infinite, magnificent,

Awe-inspiring, humbling.

He wants to talk with me-

The Great I AM

Whispers MY name-

Peace, joy, laughter-

Bubbling over

Cannot contain it.

Communion with my Savior.

No greater love.

THIRTY-EIGHT

It's a Mystery

"Can you fathom the mysteries of God? Can you probe the limits of the Almighty? They are higher than the heavens above- what can you do? They are deeper than the depths below- what can you know? Their measure is longer than the earth and wider than the sea." **Job 11:7-9**

It's a mystery

That the earth

Is the perfect distance

From the sun,

That the stars shine

In the night skies,

And the moon

Shines bright at night.

It's a mystery

That the birds sing,

Lions roar,

And Leopards

Have spots.

It's a mystery

That the oceans roar,

And the leaves

Rustle in the wind.

It's a mystery

That He created time

And then split it

In half with the

Birth of His Son.

It's a mystery

That God could love me

So much.

Selfish and full of sin

Yet forgiven

Because of his

Unconditional love.

THIRTY-NINE

Jesus

"In the beginning was the Word, and the Word was with God, and the Word was God. He was with God in the beginning. Through him all things were made; without him nothing was made that has been made. In him was life, and that life was the light of all mankind. The light shines in the darkness, and the darkness has not overcome it." **John 1:1-5**

Word become flesh,

From infinity, eternity

To finite time.

Born of a virgin,

Son of God

Crucified for our sins.

Conquering death.

He rose again.

There can be no question.

He is indeed God's one & only son-

Fulfilling prophecies of old.

There is no other

Who's done what he's done.

No one else can.

Some say he's just a great teacher,

It's just another myth,

He's crazy.

Not true!

He didn't leave that option.

He is who He claimed to be-

God's One and only Son.

The Triune God

Offering us the greatest gift of all-

Eternity with Him.

FORTY

Jesus is the Reason

"They found the stone rolled away from the tomb, but when they entered, they did not find the body of the Lord Jesus. While they were wondering about this, suddenly two men in clothes that gleamed like lightning stood beside them. In their fright the women bowed down with their faces to the ground, but the men said to them, 'Why do you look for the living among the dead: He is not here; he has risen! Remember how he told you, while he was still with you in Galilee: 'The Son of Man must be delivered over to the hands of sinners, be crucified and on the third day be raised again.'" **Luke 24:2-7**

Jesus is the reason

For the season of giving

As He gave the ultimate gift.

He was born of a virgin,

Leaving His heavenly home,

And was wrapped

In swaddling clothes.

The young family ran

And the young family hid

While God protected them from above.

As He grew and learned

He began speaking His Word

To all who would stop and listen.

The Word became flesh

Turned water into wine.

The blind now see

and the deaf can hear.

The dead were raised to new life.

The Pharisees tried to stop Him,

Judas betrayed Him,

And He was crucified high on a cross.

But the grave couldn't hold Him.

The soldiers ran in fear

As the stone was rolled away.

He arose from the dead

Ascending to God above,

Preparing a home for you and me.

FORTY-ONE

The Joy of the Lord

"Do not grieve, for the joy of the Lord is your strength." **Nehemiah 8:10b**

The joy of the Lord

Gives me strength

To make it through

Each day.

The joy of the Lord

Overwhelms and overflows,

Spilling over in worship

And devotion,

Thankfulness and gratitude

For His mercy and grace.

No matter the battle

His love surrounds me,

Flows from within me.

The joy of the Lord

Is my shield and my song.

It's the light in the darkness.

It's my sword to help

Me fight the good fight.

The joy of the Lord

Is the peace deep inside-

Directing me, teaching me,

And showing me the way.

The joy of the Lord

Is like a beacon on a hill.

You cannot miss it

As it shines for all to see.

FORTY-TWO

The King is Coming

"'Look, he is coming with the clouds,' and 'every eye will see him, even those who pierced him; and all peoples on earth 'will mourn because of him.' So shall it be! Amen. I am the Alpha and the Omega,' says the Lord God, 'who is, and who was, and who is to come, the Almighty.'"
Revelation 1:7-8

The King is coming soon

To take home His bride.

Purified through His blood,

Our sins no more reside.

The dead in Christ shall rise first

Then those alive in Him.

We're changed in an instant

Joining Him in the Sky.

And then, the end will come

Judgment and rewards

Are given as He reigns

from New Jerusalem.

As the earth is renewed,

Satan is bound.

Forever shall God reign.

Praise Jesus, Son of God

Word become Flesh,

Loving Savior, Forever King.

FORTY-THREE

King of the Universe

"The true light that gives light to everyone was coming into the world.
He was in the world, and though the world was made through him, the
world did not recognize him." **John 1: 9-10**

Blessed are you oh Lord my God,

King of the Universe!

You stepped from eternity into time

To save us from our sins and restore us

Into your heavenly kingdom.

From Awesome Almighty God to

Innocent helpless babe,

Dependent on your own creation.

You lived as a man though fully God.

Becoming the sacrifice for all our sins,

Conquering death once and for all.

Ascending back to heaven

To prepare a place for all who believe,

And accept your infinite grace and

Loving forgiveness.

Thank you, my Jesus.

You are King of Kings and Lord of Lords!

You are alone are worthy to be praised!

Forever in your presence I will be and am always

Because of your sacrifice for me.

FORTY-FOUR

Let Him Lead

"Trust in the Lord with all your heart and lean not on your own understanding; in all your ways submit to him, and he will make your paths straight." **Proverbs 3: 5-6**

Don't rely on your

Own understanding.

Instead, trust in His.

He knows all, sees all.

He won't let you down.

Trust Him with all your heart.

He will faithfully protect it.

He will guard it

And open it to His

Everlasting love.

Acknowledge him in all you do.

Give Him glory

For He is worthy.

Let His Spirit overflow

From within

Bubbling up and

Spilling over.

Take hold of his promises.

Let Him guide you.

He will lead you

In ways you cannot

See or imagine.

Get ready for the adventure

Of a living active faith

In Him who created all.

FORTY-FIVE

Life is a Journey

"Consider it pure joy, my brothers and sisters, whenever you face trials of many kinds, because you know that the testing of your faith produces perseverance. Let perseverance finish its work so that you may be mature and complete, not lacking anything." **James 1:2-8**

Life is a journey

Not just a destination.

There's more to life

Then just the goal.

It's how you get there

That gets you ready

For where you want to go.

Lessons to learn.

Faith to grow.

Learning to give

Not just receive.

More about others,

Not just about me.

He will lead me

Wherever I need to go,

Strengthening me for

What I need to do.

He has the future

In the palm of His hands.

One step at a time

He leads me,

Showing me the way.

Just do the next right thing

And trust me.

You'll be okay.

FORTY-SIX

Loneliness and Healing

"'Ask and it will be given to you; seek and you will find; knock and the door will be opened to you. For everyone who asks receives; the one who seeks finds; and to the one who knocks, the door will be opened."
Matthew 7:7-8

Loneliness, depression

Threaten to overcome my soul.

Turn to the One

Who has made you whole.

Anger and frustration

Bubble up from within.

Trust your heart to Jesus

And He will give you peace.

Grief and hopelessness

Overwhelm my heart and mind.

Release it to your Savior

And new life and peace you will find.

So many things

Take away our hope and peace.

But there is only One

Who can restore your joy

When you lay it all at His feet.

When anger and bitterness

Come and take a hold

They will crush your spirit

And never let you go

Unless you let Him in

And let Him cleanse your heart and soul.

If you do, you won't regret it.

He'll heal you and make you whole.

FORTY-SEVEN

Look and Listen

"For since the creation of the world God's invisible qualities- his eternal power and divine nature- have been clearly seen, being understood from what has been made, so that people are without excuse." **Romans 1:20**

God's love is everywhere.

His beauty has no limits.

His mercy is everlasting.

You see Him in all creation

If you only look,

If you only listen.

Majestic mountains or

Lush green rolling hills-

From where did they come?

He laid the foundations

Of the earth.

Separated day from night.

Created time itself.

The land and the seas

Are his creation

As are the lions and the lambs,

The elephants and the eagles,

And the fish of the deep.

He spoke the stars into existence

As well as the sun and moon

To give us light.

He created you and me-

From the color of my hair

To the time and place I was born.

He gave me hopes and dreams.

He is in the details.

He's all around

If you take time

To just look and listen.

FORTY-EIGHT

The Lord is Faithful

"I will proclaim the name of the Lord. Oh, praise the greatness of our God! He is the Rock, his works are perfect, and all his ways are just."
Deuteronomy 32:3-4

The Lord is faithful.

You can trust Him

With your every care.

While others disappoint

He never will.

His grace is sufficient

For every wrong

You've done.

He mercy everlasting

Through Jesus Christ

The One and only Son.

He's the answer

To your every problem.

He'll meet

Your every need.

If you only ask,

He has the answers you seek.

With His great Wisdom

He is all-knowing

And will lead you

In all your ways.

His love is

All-encompassing

And He'll draw you close

As He heals and forgives

And takes your every care away.

FORTY-NINE

Lover of My Soul

"Jesus replied: 'Love the Lord your God with all your heart and with all your soul and with all your mind.' This is the first and greatest commandment. And the second is like it: 'Love your neighbor as yourself.' All the Law and the Prophets hand on these two commandments." **Matthew 22: 37-40**

The Joy of the Lord

Bubbles up from inside

As I learn to listen,

As I learn to abide.

The joy of the Lord

Gives me strength to go on.

When life gets hard,

I start singing His songs.

I worship Him completely

With all my heart, soul and mind.

I let His love flow through me.

I let His light shine.

I take my eyes off myself

And put them back on Him.

The Lover of my soul

Renews me once again.

FIFTY

Loving Father

"Oh, the depth of the riches of the wisdom and knowledge of God!
How unsearchable are his judgments and his paths beyond tracing out!"
Romans 11:33

How do we measure

The majesty of God?

How can we quantify

His good deeds for us?

His love is infinite-

Beyond all measure.

It knows no bounds.

He is totally trustworthy.

In Him, I can always trust.

He always keeps his Word,

There is no room for doubt.

His unlimited imagination is

Evidenced in His creation.

He is all-powerful but humbled as a baby.

He is omniscient, all-knowing

Of all our thoughts and deeds

Yet loves us and died for us anyway.

He is Omnipresent- but right here

Holding my hand and listening to me

When I need him.

Words cannot express my love for you!

Jesus, Alpha, and Omega,

Everlasting Father, Prince of Peace

Mighty God, Abba Father

Daddy God.

FIFTY-ONE

Mothers

"She is clothed with strength and dignity; she can laugh at the days to come. She speaks with wisdom, and faithful instruction is on her tongue. She watches over the affairs of her household and does not eat the bread of idleness. Her children arise and call her blessed; her husband also, and he praises her:" **Proverbs 31:25-28**

Mothers are a precious gift

Sent to us from above.

They nurture us, take care of us

And give us all their love.

They feed us and teach us

Every day of our lives.

They sing us to sleep

And tuck us in at night.

They support us in all we do

And pray for us each day.

They always put us first

And help us find our way.

No matter how much I mess up,

She will always be there

Because she loves unconditionally

And for me, will always care.

FIFTY-TWO

My Heart is Christ's Home

"He has shown you, O mortal, what is good. And what does the Lord require of you? To act justly and to love mercy and to walk humbly with your God." **Micah 6:8**

My heart is Christ's home

Now and forever.

Come Lord Jesus.

Let's dine together.

Let's laugh and talk

As you direct me each day.

Residing in me, teaching me,

And showing me the way.

Come Lord Jesus,

Let's have some fun

As we work side by side

Getting things done.

Come Lord Jesus,

Let's clean up this room.

Show me how

To release it to you.

Together we will make it

Whiter than snow

As you heal me and cleanse me

Wherever we go.

Come Lord Jesus,

Please be my guest.

Let's sit by the riverside

And quietly rest.

FIFTY-THREE

My Spirit Soars

"Sing to the Lord, all the earth; proclaim his salvation day after day. Declare his glory among the nations, his marvelous deeds among all peoples. For great is the Lord and most worthy of praise; he is to be feared above all gods. For the gods of the nations are idols, but the Lord made the heavens. Splendor and majesty are before him; strength and joy are in his dwelling place." **1 Chronicles 16: 23-27**

My spirit soars

As I ponder

Your great love-

Free, unconditional.

Nothing I can do

To earn it.

I bubble up

With laughter and joy

As the Spirit's power

Rises in me.

Through Your Spirit

There is power

And true security.

There is freedom-

Adventure.

As I trust your leading

I will forever

Sing Your praises.

Eternally do you

Deserve all glory.

You are worthy

Of all my devotion.

You are worthy

Of all honor.

My heart and soul rejoice

That I am Yours-

Forever.

FIFTY-FOUR

New Life

"Do not be deceived: God cannot be mocked. A man reaps what he sows. Whoever sows to please their flesh, from the flesh will reap destruction; whoever sows to please the Spirit, from the Spirit will reap eternal life. Let us not become weary in doing good, for at the proper time we will reap a harvest if we do not give up." **Galatians 6:9**

New life is everywhere.

It starts with a seed.

Just take a look,

Open your eyes and see.

One of the biggest trees of all

Starts with the smallest seed.

It all begins with a seed-

The marigolds, daisies

And many other flowers you see.

Trees and plants,

The fruit and vegetables

We eat.

All from a seed.

Nourished and watered

With tender loving care.

In the same way,

Our faith is a seed.

Feed it, water it

And it will grow.,

Just remember,

You shall reap

All that you sow.

So, sow good seeds

Of faith, hope and peace.

Plant seeds of love

Which nourish the soul.

Plant seeds in good soil

So they'll flourish and grow.

FIFTY-FIVE

No Christmas Without Christ

"You yourselves know that these hands of mine have supplied my own needs and the needs of my companions. In everything I did, I showed you that by this kind of hard work we must help the weak, remembering the words the Lord Jesus himself said: 'It is more blessed to give than to receive.'" **Acts 20: 34-35**

There is no Christmas

Without Christ Jesus

The Anointed One.

It's the spirit of giving-

Not so much receiving.

Follow His example

Of unconditional love.

Reach out.

Be a blessing.

Give someone

A song to sing.

Fill others with hope,

With the message of peace.

Money, presents, things

Don't matter.

Only the greatest

Gift of all

New life in Jesus-

The reason for the season.

FIFTY-SIX

No Greater Love

"Father, forgive them, for they do not know what they are doing." **Luke 23:34**

Lord, when you chose your disciples,

You chose one whom you knew would betray you.

At the last supper, you told him to go,

Knowing what he was about to do.

In the Garden of Gethsemane,

when the soldiers came, you did not resist.

When questioned by the Pharisees,

You did not defend yourself.

When asked if you were the Messiah,

You simply stated, "Yes, I am He"-

In their minds blasphemy.

When questioned by Herod,

He had you scourged.

You still did not resist.

When mocked by the soldiers,

Still, you said nothing.

When Pilate questioned you,

You said nothing except to confirm

that you were a king and to tell him

The only power he had over you

Was given to him from above.

After being beaten and mocked and flogged,

You still did nothing,

Even knowing that at any time

You could have called down

Twelve legions of angels to help you.

Throughout all of this,

You never wavered,

You were always true-

Even when you hung on the cross and said:

"Father, forgive them

For they know not what they do."

My love for you cannot ever compare

To your love for me.

FIFTY-SEVEN

No More Striving

"Come to me, all you who are weary and burdened, and I will give you rest. Take my yoke upon you and learn from me, for I am gentle and humble in heart, and you will find rest for your souls. For my yoke is easy and my burden is light." **Matthew 11:28-30**

Fighting, resisting

Striving to do it on my own.

Stress, fear, and doubts

Cloud my heart and mind.

How to release it?

How to surrender?

Lay it all down

At the feet of Jesus.

His blood cleanses,

Heals, forgives.

He raises me up.

Takes my burdens

As His own.

Have faith and trust.

One step at a time.

He's in control.

He'll carry your every burden

And bring you peace.

Trust God and do

The next right thing.

FIFTY-EIGHT

No Need to Worry

"And we know that in all things God works for the good of those who love him, who have been called according to his purpose." **Romans 8:28**

No need to worry.

No need to fear.

He takes my mistakes

And works them for good.

Everything old

Is made new again.

Water is turned into wine

And food is multiplied.sin-filled

The blind now see,

The deaf hear

And dead are raised

To new life.

Our sin-filled hearts

Are cleansed and

The Holy Spirit now lives within.

We're renewed

Day by day.

And one day soon,

The earth too

Will be renewed

When He returns

With New Jerusalem.

Streets of gold

And the river of life,

No more evil, death, or disease-

Just the life-giving

Light of God

For all eternity.

Fifty-Nine

Nowhere

"Where can I go from your Spirit? Where can I flee from your presence? If I go up to the heavens, you are there; if I make my bed in the depths, you are there. If I rise on the wings of the dawn, if I settle on the far side of the sea, even there your hand will guide me, your right hand will hold me fast." **Psalms 139:7-10**

There is nowhere

I can go

Where God cannot find me.

He is everywhere.

If I hide in the darkest cave

He is there.

If I am lost in the crowd-

He finds me.

He watches over me

As I sleep

And guides my steps

Each day as I awake.

He knows my every need

Before I ever speak.

He waits for me

To ask for help-

To see my faith,

To take hold of His promises.

He's waiting for me.

Protecting me.

Surrounding me with His love.

He'll never ever leave me.

He'll never let me go.

No matter what I've done

His love is true.

Unconditional.

He heals my soul.

SIXTY

On That Christmas Day

"The Word became flesh and made his dwelling among us. We have seen his glory, the glory of the one and only Son, who came from the Father, full of grace and truth." **John 1:14**

On that Christmas Day

So very long ago

A Savior King was born.

He came from heaven.

He lived on earth.

He died and rose again.

He came to earth to suffer.

And for us, He came to die.

He came to show us the way.

He was arrested and tried.

He was whipped and hung high.

And died for the sins of the world.

They cast lots for His clothes

And from his side

His blood flowed.

Was buried in a tomb

And the stone rolled in place.

A rumbling was soon heard

As God showed the world

That Jesus had risen from the grave.

The price was now paid

Once and for all

For those who choose to believe.

He's coming back soon

For to take home His bride.

Home to Heaven

Where He's prepared a place.

Forever we'll be by His side.

SIXTY-ONE

Once I was lost

"Are not five sparrows sold for two pennies? Yet not one of them is forgotten by God. Indeed, the very hairs of our head are all numbered. Don't be afraid; you are worth more than many sparrows." **Luke 12: 6-7**

Once I was lost.

But now I am found.

I was blind

But now I see.

How could He love

Such a sinner like me

Is more than I can see.

You died in my place

And extended me grace

And then you rose again.

You went to prepare

A home for your bride

And soon I'll see you again.

It was all about me

When you died on that day

And now you'll forever

Be praised.

SIXTY-TWO

One Voice

"My sheep listen to my voice; I know them, and they follow Me. I give them eternal life, and they shall never perish; no one will snatch them out of my hand." **John 10:27**

So many voices, but not the One I need.

Only one voice has the answers I seek.

No answers are found in voices

Other than the One.

Not in media, celebrities, or web,

Parents, church, or self.

Only the Father, Spirit, and Son- 3 in 1-

Can speak the words I need to hear.

Sometimes in a burning bush,

Sometimes through a donkey.

Sometimes loud and unmistakable,

Sometimes but a whisper that I strain to hear.

Many forms but One voice the same.

With one voice we worship

The One who is above all.

Omniscient, omnipotent and Omnipresent.

My loving Savior and God.

Sixty-Three

Overflowing

"May the Lord make your love increase and overflow for each other and for everyone else, just as ours does for you." **1 Thessalonians 3:12**

Your love is overwhelming

Like a cup

That runneth over.

Your joy overflowing

Like a waterfall.

There is no room

To contain it.

A thankful heart.

For Your grace,

Mercy, and Your touch.

Flow through me.

Anoint me

Into your service,

Spilling over to others.

Healing hearts.

Healing souls.

Healing bodies.

Draw them into

Your wide embrace.

There's room for all

To walk the narrow way.

I will be Your witness.

I will go.

May Your love, joy,

Peace, and healing

Spill over

To draw others

Into Your eternal kingdom-

My all in all-

Jesus.

SIXTY-FOUR

Peace! Be Still!

"You will keep in perfect peace those whose minds are steadfast, because they trust in you. Trust in the Lord forever, for the Lord, the Lord himself, is the Rock eternal." **Isaiah 26:3-4**

Peace! Be still!

Listen for my voice

And, you, I will lead.

I will strengthen you

And hold you

And teach you my ways.

I'll never, ever leave you

But will always love you.

You're my child, my bride,

My love is deep and wide.

Everlasting.

Never ending.

Eternally you are mine

In this world and the next.

I will give you rest.

Peace, be still, and listen.

SIXTY-FIVE

Perfectly

"For God so loved the world that he gave his one and only Son, that whoever believes in him shall not perish but have eternal life. For God did not send his Son into the world to condemn the world, but to save the world through him." **John 3:16-17**

My hope is in the Lord

From which I came.

He saved my soul

And redeemed my shame.

I'll live for Him

And I'll die for Him.

I'll share His love

And I'll share His light.

He's my hope, my peace

My everything.

He saves me and heals me

And leads me each step of the way.

He never leaves me

And will never forsake me.

He loves me unconditionally

No matter the mistakes I make.

He will never let me go

And will never turn His back.

It's not possible-

He's perfect in every way.

He's perfectly good and perfectly righteous.

He's my perfect loving Savior

And loves ME Perfectly.

SIXTY-SIX

Pray the Name

"and his incomparably great power for us who believe. That power is the same as the mighty strength he exerted when he raised Christ from the dead and seated him at his right hand in the heavenly realms, far above all rule and authority, power and dominion, and every name that is invoked, not only in the present age but also in the one to come. And God placed all things under his feet and appointed him to be head over everything for the church, which is his body, the fullness of him who fills everything in every way." **Ephesians 1:19-23**

Pray the name of Jesus.

He's waiting for your prayer.

You have only to ask.

He wants you to share.

There's power in His name

And in His blood, there is healing.

He'll meet your every need

And knows exactly what you're feeling.

Nothing will surprise Him

For He knows it all.

He's waiting with open arms.

He'll never let you fall.

There's authority in His name.

Stand firm and be bold.

In Him, you're more than a conqueror

And His love's more precious than gold.

SIXTY-SEVEN

Preparation

"For you, God, tested us; you refined us like silver. You brought us into prison and laid burdens on our backs. You let people ride over our heads; we went through fire and water, but you brought us to a place of abundance." **Psalms 66:10-12**

I know the end is soon.

There isn't much time.

I seek to hear His voice

To discern what to do next.

I know I am certainly

In the midst of a test.

But then isn't that what this life is?

A series of tests?

It's preparation for the next life

For life in eternity.

Forever with my Savior,

Serving Him daily.

Not just cloud sitting

Or watching clouds in the sky.

But purpose In Christ.

In Him is our identity.

Forever growing, worshipping.

Forever- just being with Him.

Grow now, learn to trust.

Feed the spirit deep within.

SIXTY-EIGHT

Press In

"I remain confident of this: I will see the goodness of the Lord in the land of the living. Wait for the Lord; be strong and take heart and wait for the Lord." **Psalms 27:13-14**

Press into God.

You are above all.

First in my life.

Strip me to the bone.

Take it all.

I need nothing but You.

All else pales in comparison.

Lead me in your ways.

I know nothing.

Everything I am

I give to you

For your purpose,

Your way.

SIXTY-NINE

The Rose

"But God demonstrates his own love for us in this: While we were still sinners, Christ died for us." **Romans 5:8**

The love of God is unconditional

And fragrant like a rose.

It fills the senses.

Is freely given.

But not without cost.

He wore a crown of thorns

On that world-changing day.

They pierced His flesh.

His blood flowed.

Cleansing us from all sin.

His fragrant offering

Fills the senses,

Like that of a rose.

Beauty overflowing.

Love spilling over.

A symbol of love

And how much it costs.

Paying the ultimate price

To restore us to himself.

Eternally.

SEVENTY

Salt & Light

"You are the salt of the earth. But if the salt loses its saltiness, how can it be made salty again? It is no longer good for anything, except to be thrown out and trampled underfoot. "You are the light of the world. A town built on a hill cannot be hidden. Neither do people light a lamp and put it under a bowl. Instead, they put it on its stand, and it gives light to everyone in the house. In the same way, let your light shine before others, that they may see your good deeds and glorify your Father in heaven."
Matthew 5: 13-16

Darkness, shadows

Struggle to stifle the light.

Be salt and light

In a world of shadows.

We are called His children.

In the world

Not of the world.

In the world

To be a light

As He is the light.

His love lights the darkness,

Dispels the shadows.

So should we.

Raise your sights

And be His light

In this fallen world.

Soon to be redeemed,

He's coming soon

For His bride.

Be ready and shine a light.

Show His love.

Dispel the shadows.

Be the light

As He is the light.

SEVENTY-ONE

See My Heart

"In their hearts humans plan their course, but the Lord establishes his steps." **Proverbs 16:9**

Jesus, Savior,

Coming King,

My best friend,

Hear my cry.

See my heart.

I worship you

King of kings,

Lord of Lords..

My heart song is

Your will,

Your way,

Your Word,

To be your witness.

Give me eyes to see.

Give me ears to hear.

Lead me.

Speak through me

Use me.

Your plan.

Your purpose.

May it be accomplished.

May it be fulfilled.

Totally,

Completely,

Through Jesus -

In His name.

Amen.

SEVENTY-TWO

Seek Him First

"But seek first his kingdom and his righteousness, and all these things will be given to you as well." **Matthew 6:33**

Fame and fortune,

Money, power, and status.

Greed.

Silver and gold,

Expensive cars.

Million-dollar homes.

Things of this world-

Meaningless.

Where does your heart

Truly lie?

Where is your treasure?

On things of earth?

Or, on those of heaven?

Seek first God's kingdom

Then all else will follow.

He knows what you need.

He'll provide it all

And so much more

If you put Him first

In your heart

And in all you do.

SEVENTY-THREE

Shaped By the Potter's Hand

"Yet you, Lord, are our Father. We are the clay, you are the potter; we are all the work of your hand." **Isaiah 64:8**

I'm shaped by the Potter's hand

Before time began.

He molds me and makes me

Into who He created me to be.

His loving hands shape me,

Helping me to be all that He

Wants me to be.

His vision is perfect.

There are no mistakes.

He created me to be a light

He created me with purpose

For a purpose-

To share his love

The story of new life.

He created me to love him

And just be with him.

He created me to be

Loved by him,

For relationship, and

Fellowship.

What are the dreams

Deep within me?

He shaped those too.

Everything about me

From the color of my hair

To where and when I was born

Was planned before time.

I'm shaped by the Master Potter.

His love guides me

Each step of the way.

His love fills me and

Helps me understand

Just who He created me to be.

SEVENTY-FOUR

Sin and Temptation

"For the flesh desires what is contrary to the Spirit, and the Spirit what is contrary to the flesh. They are in conflict with each other, so that you are not to do whatever you want. But if you are led by the Spirit, you are not under the law." **Galatians 5:17-18**

Sin and temptation

Surround me on every side.

I want to resist,

To do what is right

But don't have the strength

To do it on my own.

You died to save me,

To heal me, and forgive me.

You died to make me whole.

Please give me the strength

To continue the fight,

Resisting temptation

With You by my side.

The Holy Spirit within

And wisdom from Your

Holy Word.

SEVENTY-FIVE

So Much Need

"He heals the brokenhearted and binds up their wounds." **Psalms 147: 3**

So much need.

So many broken hearts.

Hunger.

Grief.

Loss.

Homelessness.

Lay your burdens

On Jesus.

Come to Him

And find rest.

Find peace.

Let Him take your pain,

Your heartache.

Lay it all on Him.

He is faithful.

Trustworthy.

Gently will He heal you.

With His strength,

He will raise you up.

With His Wisdom

Will He guide you

In righteous paths.

He is the great Provider

And will see to your every need.

Trust Him

Who is totally trustworthy.

Put your faith in Him

Who died in your place.

SEVENTY-SIX

So Thankful

"The LORD Almighty has sworn, "Surely, as I have planned, so it will be, and as I have purposed, so it will happen." **Isaiah 14:24**

Nothing physical,

But, oh so much eternal.

No tree with presents,

But the greatest gift of all-

Jesus, Savior.

Finances slim.

But God is in control.

His purpose prevails.

Always.

Ready to release His power,

His Spirit.

No need to understand.

Just be ready to say "Yes."

Ready to go forth

Into the new year,

Into the world.

His saint, His servant.

So much to be thankful for-

Jesus, John

His provision,

His leading,

Grace, forgiveness, and power.

Jesus-

King of Kings and

Lord of Lords.

SEVENTY-SEVEN

A Soldier in God's Army

"Therefore, put on the full armor of God, so that when the day of evil comes, you may be able to stand your ground, and after you have done everything, to stand." **Ephesians 6:13**

I'm a soldier in God's Army.

Ready to fight

And share the light.

Fully alive through the

The blood of Jesus Christ.

Forgiven and redeemed,

Daughter of God Almighty,

King of the Universe.

"Yes, Lord," I say

"Lead the way."

Surrendered to you

In all that I do.

To honor you with my life

And share your light

Is what I want most to do.

You alone are worthy.

The whole world sings of your glory.

May your light shine through me

As you teach me to be

All that you've created me to be.

SEVENTY-EIGHT

Soon

"Look, I am coming soon! My reward is with me, and I will give to each person according to what they have done." **Revelation 22:12**

The end is near.

He's coming soon

In clouds of glory

To take his bride home.

Tribulations first-

Persecution,

Mark of the Beast,

Antichrist reigns.

So subtle at first-

Chips in the hand

Disguised in the form

Of convenience.

Don't be deceived!

Stand strong!

Jesus first!

The only true king-

Lord of lords.

He'll be here soon-

Sooner than you expect.

Wake up sleeping church!

Put on your armor!

Root out evil!

Repent and be forgiven!

Not much time left-

He's coming again-

Soon.

SEVENTY-NINE

The Storm Rages

"The Lord is my strength and my shield; my heart trusts in him, and he helps me. My heart leaps for joy, and with my song I praise him." **Psalms 28:7**

The winds howl and rage outside

But He keeps me safe in His arms.

Joy still fills my heart

For He keeps me from all harm.

The waves rise higher and higher

But He shields me on every side.

The storm threatens to overcome me

But He gives me peace inside.

No storm shall prevail against me

Because He loves me so.

No matter how it looks

He is always in control.

EIGHTY

Storms of Life

"Then they cried out to the Lord in their trouble, and he brought them out of their distress. He stilled the storm to a whisper; the waves of the sea were hushed. They were glad when it grew calm, and he guided them to their desired haven." **Psalms 107:28-30**

As the storms

Come at me

From every side,

You're my anchor.

You keep me safe.

You keep me secure.

When darkness threatens

To overwhelm my soul,

Your light pierces

Every corner of my heart.

Your light spills over

With joy overflowing.

When I'm worn and weary

And don't have

The strength to go on,

You lift me up and carry me.

You give me rest

For my soul.

When I'm wrapped up in fear

And my faith is small,

I call on you and your answer

And Your peace takes it all.

When grief overcomes me

And I don't know

How to go on,

Your arms envelop me

With Your everlasting love.

EIGHTY-ONE

The Sun Rises

"I am the Lord, and there is no other; apart from me there is no God. I will strengthen you, though you have not acknowledged me, so that from the rising of the sun to the place of its setting people may know there is none besides me, I am the Lord, and there is no other. I form the light and create darkness, I bring prosperity and create disaster; I, the Lord, do all these things." **Isaiah 45:5-7**

The sun rises

Each new and glorious day.

Full of new hope,

New life, new possibilities.

Don't know what will come.

But I know He's in control.

I just trust and listen

For the still small voice within.

Step out in faith

And obey the Son

Who also rose

Once and for all.

Paying the price

To give us new life

And free us from sin.

The sun sets

With a brilliant display.

Rainbows of colors

No two are the same.

This day is done

But a new one

Will soon begin

More brilliant than before.

Streets of gold

And gates of solid pearls

More Incredible

Then I can imagine.

My new and future home.

EIGHTY-TWO

Sweet, Sweet Surrender

"Then he said to them all: 'Whoever wants to be my disciple must deny themselves and take up their cross daily and follow me." **Luke 9:23**

Sweet, sweet surrender

Of all that I am

To the One that knows me best.

He knows who I was.

He knows who I am.

And I know He knows what's best.

He is the potter

And I am the clay.

He'll mold me and shape me

As we walk together each day.

He will lead

And I will follow.

Together we'll go side by side.

He will teach and I will learn.

He'll open my heart.

And open my eyes

To all the possibilities

He's placed deep inside.

He'll speak and I will listen

To that still small voice within.

And, together we'll create

Beautiful, wondrous things,

Rejoicing for we're working

Together side by side

In harmony with my Savior

In whom I forever abide.

EIGHTY-THREE

Thank You, Lord

"Rejoice always, pray continually, give thanks in all circumstances; for this is God's will for you in Christ Jesus." **1 Thessalonians 5:16**

Thank you, Lord,

For the love you've given me.

Thank you, Lord,

For forever forgiving me.

Thank you, Lord,

For your Holy Spirit deep within.

Thank you, Lord,

For joy and laughter

Bubbling from within.

Thank you, Lord,

For providing for all my needs.

Thank you, Lord,

That if I look and listen

I know you will lead.

Thank you, Lord,

For miracles big and small.

Thank you, Lord,

That you pick me up

Every time I fall.

Thank you, Lord,

For my husband

Who loves me so much.

Thank you, Lord,

For birds and squirrels

And kitties and such.

Thank you, Lord,

For friends old and new.

Thank you, Lord,

That in Jesus we are renewed.

Thank you, Lord,

For peace, hope, and love.

Thank you, Lord,

For your mercy from above.

Thank you, Lord,

For justice and truth

Which I now know

Is found only in You.

Thank you, Lord,

For creation and beauty everywhere.

Thank you, Lord,

For love to share.

Thank you, Lord,

That your love

Is fragrant as a rose.

Thank you, Lord,

That you died for me

And then arose.

EIGHTY-FOUR

To Whom Do I Belong?

"For none of us lives for ourselves alone, and none of us dies for ourselves alone. If we live, we live for the Lord; ad if we die, we die for the Lord. So, whether we live or die, we belong to the Lord. For this very reason, Christ died and returned to life so that he might be the Lord of both the dead and the living." **Romans 14:7-9**

I belong to Jesus

Who sits on the throne,

Reigning from Heaven

And preparing a home.

He came to earth

And bore my sins,

Restoring my soul and

Making me new again.

He descended to hell

Paying the price

To restore me to Himself

And bring me new life.

Forever my heart

Will sing for joy

At the wondrous gift

I can now enjoy.

Eternally with Him

In my new home,

In heaven above

With Jesus on the throne.

EIGHTY-FIVE

Transformed

"Now the Lord is the Spirit, and where the Spirit of the Lord is, there is freedom. And we all, who with unveiled faces contemplate the Lord's glory, are being transformed into his image with ever-increasing glory, which comes from the Lord, who is the Spirit." **2 Corinthians 3:17-18**

I'm transformed, renewed

From the inside out.

Saved once, born again

But change continues within.

The Holy Spirit works

One day at a time,

Changing my heart

And renewing my mind.

Cleaning out the closets

Where pain and hurt are buried.

Shining a light on the darkness

There's no more need to hide.

Showing me who

He created me to be.

I'm learning to trust,

To listen, and just be.

It's not all about doing,

But so much more about being.

Just taking time daily

To spend time with Him.

Beginning to understand

That if I trust He will lead.

Learning to walk side by side.

Listening and growing

As in my Lord, I abide.

It's a process never-ending,

Continuing to grow and change.

He's molding me and shaping me

Into who He created me to be.

EIGHTY-SIX

Trials

"In all this you greatly rejoice, though now for a little while you may have had to suffer grief in all kinds of trials. These have come so that the proven genuineness of your faith- of greater worth than gold, which perishes even though refined by fire- may result in praise, glory and honor when Jesus Christ is revealed. Though you have not seen Him, you love Him; and even though you do not see Him now, you believe in Him and are filled with an inexpressible and glorious joy, for you are receiving the end result of your faith, the salvation of your souls." **1 Peter 1:6-9**

In life there are trials

But He'll see us through.

Each one is a chance

To learn something new,

To discover of what

You are made,

And in whom you will

Place your faith.

Will you give up

Will you give in

Or will you trust God

Who will help you win?

The journey is more important

Then reaching the goal.

It's where you learn who you are

And reconcile your own soul.

It won't be easy

But it is worthwhile

To trust that God

Will see you through this trial.

EIGHTY-SEVEN

The Ultimate Price

"Greater love has no one than this: to lay down one's life for one's friends."
John 15:13

There is no greater love

Than that of God above.

He forgives our every sin

And wraps us in His love.

He bled and He died

And paid the ultimate price.

Forgave my many sins

And gave me new life.

From hell, He redeemed my soul.

Now He's forever

Made me whole.

Restored once and for all

To My God, Jesus,

My heavenly home.

EIGHTY-EIGHT

Walk On Water

"'Lord, if it's you,' Peter replied, 'tell me to come to you on the water.' 'Come,' he said. Then Peter got down out of the boar, walked on the water and came toward Jesus. But when he saw the wind, he was afraid and, beginning to sink, cried out, 'Lord, save me!' Immediately Jesus reached out his hand and caught him. 'You of little faith,' he said, 'why did you doubt?'" **Matthew 14:28- 31**

Walk on water.

Take a step of faith.

Keep your eyes on Jesus.

He will always keep you safe.

Take a walk on the water.

Trust His mighty power.

Nothing will overcome you

For He is your strong tower.

Take a walk on the water.

Trust Him as He calls.

He'll never, ever leave you.

He'll never let you fall.

EIGHTY-NINE

Water

"but whoever drinks the water I give them will never thirst. Indeed, the water I give them will become in them a spring of water welling up to eternal life." **John 4:14**

Water-

Reflective

Like a mirror.

Cooling.

Soothing

Like a soft breeze.

Playful

Like a dolphin.

Beautiful.

Awe Inspiring

Like a sunset.

Heart Warming

Like a child's laugh.

Peaceful.

Refreshing

Like God's Holy Spirit.

Cleansing

Like the blood of Jesus.

Life Giving,

Powerful

Like God's love.

NINETY

What is Love?

"Love is patient, love is kind. It does not envy, it does not boast, it is not proud. It does not dishonor others, it is not self-seeking. It is not easily angered, it keeps no record of wrongs. Love does not delight in evil but rejoices with the truth. It always protects, always trusts, always hopes, always perseveres." **1 Corinthians 13: 4-7**

What is love?

The word is thrown around

All the time.

But, what does it really mean?

It's a generous act of kindness.

A selfless sacrifice.

A kind word spoken

To someone in need.

It is patient and forgiving.

It doesn't envy or boast.

Others are put first.

There are no conditions

On true Agape love.

It's peace where there is strife.

Gentleness when one is broken.

Quiet strength in the midst

Of opposition.

It's standing strong,

Willing to sacrifice for

A purpose greater than your own

It's Jesus leaving his home

In heaven,

Coming to suffer and die

On the cross

For your sins and my own.

NINETY-ONE

What's Your Story?

"A person's steps are directed by the Lord. How then can anyone understand their own way?" **Proverbs 20:24**

What's your story?

We all have one you know.

We all have a tale to tell.

We all have something to show.

There is always a way

To show the love you know.

A smile on your face

Or extending forgiveness

And grace.

Do you know the Father?

Do you know the Son?

Remember Him in your heart

Each morning as the day's begun.

What's your story?

How has He blessed your life?

In so many ways

Both big and small.

People, provision, and protection.

Opportunities, skills, forgiveness.

He saves us, heals us and

Provides a heavenly home.

His mercy is never-ending.

His love for you is perfect.

He loves you just as you are.

Designed you to be unique.

So, what's your story?

Who did He create you to be?

What did He put in your heart?

How has He blessed your life?

Salvation?

Forgiveness?

Healing?

What's your story?

He's given you one, you know.

NINETY-TWO

Where is Freedom?

"Heaven and earth will pass away, but my words will never pass away. But about that day or hour no one knows, not even the angels in heaven, nor the Son, but only the Father. As it was in the days of Noah, so it will be at the coming of the Son of Man." **Matthew 24: 35-37**

Where is freedom?

Where can it be found?

In a nine-to-five?

Or, with money and power?

In security?

But what does that mean?

A steady paycheck

Or a beautiful home?

Power or position?

Status and fame?

Who do you know?

What things do you claim?

Where do you find rest?

Only one true source.

In the Spirit of the Lord

Is true freedom found.

In Jesus Christ

Is security and rest.

This world is not our home.

Only your spirit and soul

Last forever, you know.

All else will fade away.

Where do you want

Your eternal home to be?

NINETY-THREE

Who Am I?

"Because you are his sons, God sent the Spirit of his Son into our hearts, the Spirit who calls out, 'Abba', Father.' So you are no longer a slave, but God's child; and since you are his child, God has made you also an heir."
Galatians 4:6-7

Who am I?

Before I was born

You knew my name.

You are the potter.

I am the clay.

You created me on purpose

Just the way I am

For a purpose.

From the color of my eyes

To my dreams and skills,

From my talents and abilities

To my parents,

I am created to be your light,

To reflect Your glory.

Wherever I may be,

I am your Child.

Forgiven by Your grace.

Restored thru the blood of Jesus.

Out of darkness

And into the light.

I am eternal.

From God I came

And to God I will return.

I AM the church.

I AM the Body of Christ.

NINETY-FOUR

Why?

"For we are God's handiwork, created in Christ Jesus to do good works, which God prepared in advance for us to do." **Ephesians 2:10**

Why did I die

Before I had the chance to live?

Why didn't you want me?

Did I do something wrong?

Why didn't I get the chance

To see the mountains?

To play in the ocean

Or feel the wind on my face?

To taste chocolate or

To know what it is to love?

To make angels in the snow

Or smell the fresh mountain air?

Who was I supposed to be?

A doctor who finds the cure for cancer?

A musician who blesses others with her music?

A police officer who saves someone's life?

A mother?

A wife?

Dancer?

Actor?

Preacher?

I'll never know-

I never got the chance to live.

NINETY-FIVE

The World is Changing

"'Let us rejoice and be glad and give him glory! For the wedding of the Lamb has come, and his bride has made herself ready. Fine Linen, bright and clean, was given her to wear.' (Fine linen, stands for the righteous acts of God's holy people) Then the angel said to me, 'Write this: Blessed are those who are invited to the wedding supper of the Lamb!' And he added, 'These are the true words of God.'" **Revelation 19:7-9**

The world is changing

Right before my eyes.

The end times,

Book of Revelation,

Come to life.

Evil is now good

And good is evil.

It's all around.

Only in Jesus

Can hope be found.

God is coming soon

To take home His bride.

Judgment too-

There's no place to hide.

Make your choice-

The end is now near.

Eternity below-

Away from all that's good.

Or, eternity with God

In love, joy, and peace.

In eternal paradise

NINETY-SIX

Worn and Weary

"For I am convinced that neither death nor life, neither angels nor demons, neither the present nor the future, nor any powers, neither height nor depth, no anything else in all creation, will be able to separate us from the love of God that is in Christ Jesus our Lord." **Romans 8:38-39**

Tired of this world.

Ready for the next.

Worn and weary.

Wanting rest for my soul.

Only in Jesus

Can my spirit find peace.

Lead me beside still waters.

Hold my hand.

Hold my heart, and

Keep me safe

From the storms of life.

Let me rest in your

Everlasting love.

Let me rest in your

Loving arms.

Never will you leave me.

Never will you forsake me.

One day I will be with you

Forever, in eternity.

Until then I know that

Nothing will ever separate me

From your everlasting, unending love.

NINETY-SEVEN

Worn Out

"Do you not know? Have you not heard? The Lord is the everlasting God, the Creator of the ends of the earth. He will not grow tired or weary, and his understanding no one can fathom. He gives strength to the weary and increases the power of the weak. Even youths grow tired and weary, and young men stumble and fall; but those who hope in the Lord will renew their strength. They will soar on wings like eagles; they will run and not grow weary, they will walk and not be faint." **Isaiah 40:28-31**

I'm tired and frustrated

Worn out from the fight

Will it never end?

Is there an end in sight?

I need you and want you

To come renew my soul.

Please come to me, Lord.

Please make me whole.

I pray for your peace.

I pray for your light.

Fill me, and surround me

With your never-ending light.

It's only in you

That any hope can be found.

It's only in you

That I can no longer be bound.

Fear, fatigue, and bitterness

No longer have a hold

Because you're always with me

Because you made me whole.

NINETY-EIGHT

Worry

"There is no fear in love, but perfect love drives out fear, because fear has to do with punishment. The one who fears is not made perfect in love."
1John 4:18

Worry,

Fear,

Unpaid bills.

Unknown future.

How to get through?

Confusion.

Need hope.

Need peace.

"Fear not."

Says Jesus.

But how?

"Trust me"

He says.

"Lay it down,

Perfect love casts out

All fears."

Yes, Lord.

I will.

Peace.

NINETY-NINE

You Can't Fight the Darkness

"You, Lord, keep my lamp burning; my God turns my darkness into light."
Psalms 18:28

You can't fight the darkness

With darkness.

It only creates more.

The harder I fight it,

The more control it seems to have.

Instead, fill the darkness

With the light of God.

If you fill the darkness

With light,

The darkness disappears

What is light?

Jesus on a cross.

True, unconditional love.

ONE HUNDRED

You're Almost There

"Not that I have already obtained all this, or have already arrived at my goal but I press on to take hold of that for which Christ Jesus took hold of me. Brothers and sisters, I do not consider myself yet to have taken hold of it. But one thing I do: Forgetting what is behind and straining toward what is ahead, I press on toward the goal to win the prize for which God has called me heavenward in Christ Jesus." **Philippians 3:12-14**

You're almost there.

Don't give up yet.

Let the Spirit lead you

For on you His eyes are set.

Don't stop short.

Trust the Savior of your soul.

He's right by your side

And will help you reach the goal.

Look deep within

You know you're not done.

Draw on His strength

Don't rely on your own.

His power is infinite.

His resources too.

Let Him help, let Him lead

And there's nothing you can't do.

You can do it

Just don't give up.

Remember your salvation

And drink of His Cup.

About Author

Patricia Grace Adderley is a former missionary and actress. It was while serving as a missionary in a Christian repertory theater company called the Covenant Players that she first started to write. When writing poetry, it is often like the Psalms- a combination of prayers and worship. It's an outpouring of her heart in the moment.

Having struggled with identity and self-worth issues while growing up, She has now become an advocate for helping other people understand that they have a true identity that is based on the Bible. One that is based on who God created them to be and what Jesus did on the cross for us 2,000 years ago.

She seeks to inspire people in their walk with God. She wants her writing to be inspirational, thought-provoking, and encouraging.

Patricia now has four books to her credit including *Finding Peace in Jesus: An Encouraging 30 Day Devotional, Loving Jesus: A 30 Day Devotional,*
Discover Your True Identity: A 52 Week Guided Prayer Journal, and One Year of Daily Creative Writing Prompts.

Patricia now lives in the beautiful state of Florida with her husband, John.

www.facebook.com/patriciagadderley/

www.pinterest.com/patriciaadderle

For a Limited Time, Get a Free Copy of My Book

Finding Peace in Jesus: An Encouraging 30 Day Devotional

https://dl.bookfunnel.com/nl4rxrd4oh

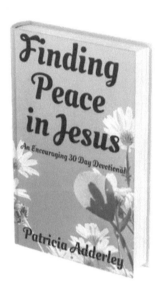

Also By Patricia Adderley

https://patriciaadderley.com/my-writing/

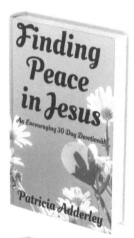

Other Resources

By Crossprint Publications

https:https://amzn.to/3FWx082

Made in United States
Troutdale, OR
10/11/2023

13611882R00126